School Journey to the Centre of the Earth

A play

Daisy Campbell with Ken Campbell

Samuel French — London
www.samuelfrench-london.co.uk

SCHOOL JOURNEY TO THE CENTRE OF THE EARTH

First presented by Stokesley School, Middlesborough as part of the Shell Connections Festival at the National Theatre, London on 18th July 2006.

BILLING REQUIREMENT

The following credit is to be given in programmes for all future performances:

"This play was commissioned by the National Theatre for 'National Theatre Connections' ".

AUTHOR'S NOTE

When you come across a reference to a TV show, advert or celebrity, please update it to reflect current popular culture (right now there would be lots of posturing like Usain Bolt). Likewise if there are great slang words that you know, please update these (go for the silly-sounding ones, rather than just plain rude).

For the Müller advert scene, pick a current advert that has a really catchy tune (right now I would choose the "We Buy Any Car" ad) and learn it off by heart, so it can be acted out exactly.

In other words, the play should always feel like it was written yesterday. Good luck!

Daisy Campbell

COPYRIGHT INFORMATION

(See also page ii)

Children and Performance Legislation

For any productions utilising children, producers will need to be aware of the appropriate child safeguarding and children in performance legislation in place. For details of the requirements you should contact your local County Council child performance advisor.

CHARACTERS

THE GIRLS:

Stacey, 8¾
Bee, 9 next Tuesday
Chrissy, same as Stacey
Miracle, 9
Anna, 9 in 21 days
Tricia, 8¾ and a bit
Jenelle, 9 this week

THE BOYS:

Sonny, 8¼
Rab, 9 last week
James, just 9
Sam, unknown
Ben, 8½
Tom, 10 in 3 weeks
Matthew, nearly 9

Miss Sheehan, class teacher of 4S (voice only)

Please note, Miss Sheehan is usually performed as a disembodied voice via a microphone from off stage. The other characters may be played by school children from Year 6 upwards.

The action of the play takes place outside and on board the school bus to Alton Towers.

Time — The Present

SCHOOL JOURNEY TO THE CENTRE OF THE EARTH

The morning of Class 4S's trip to Alton Towers. Outside the coach

The children are on stage. There is chaos: singing, skipping, fighting, dancing, screaming etc.

Stacey That ain't fair, Bee. You promised me three weeks ago that I could sit next to you on the coach.
Bee Yeah, but I promised Chrissy four weeks ago.

Stacey storms off

Stacey (*storming off*) That ain't fair. I'm telling Miss.
Chrissy Whatever. (*To Miracle*) See *X Factor* yesterday?
Miracle (*defensively*) Yeah.
Chrissy I can't believe we're gonna miss it today. Who do you reckon is gonna get kicked off?
Miracle Umm, well, what is it again? Is it the boyband or ——
Chrissy Uh no. Do you even know who's left?
Bee (*butting in*) Ohmigod what about Jamie? He is like sooooooo buff.
Anna Ohmigod!
Miracle Hey maybe there's tellies at Alton Towers.
Rab (*butting in*) They should do *X Factor* crossed with [violent video game]. (*He does an elaborate impression of someone singing horribly and then being slaughtered viciously. In a soppy voice*) Oh Jamie I love you. But now you are just mashed up into blood and bones.
Chrissy Shup Rab.
James Rah that's bare good, Rab.

*

Tricia Oh Sonny! I thought you weren't gonna make it!
Sonny My mum had another party last night. I only got her into bed at like, past midnight.
Jenelle (*to Tricia*) I'm having the window seat.
Tricia Bloody not.
Jenelle (*doing hip head wagging à la Jerry Springer*) Girlfriend, put it like this: I don't get the window seat, you don't get to sit next to me. Oh hi, Sonny.

Sonny (*to Tricia*) Is Jenelle sitting with us?
Tricia Yep.
Sonny Can I tell you a huge secret? No, forget it.
Tricia Sonny, you're my best friend. I tell you all my secrets.
Sonny Do best friend shake on it.

They do an elaborate handshake

You promise you'll never tell?
Tricia Cross my heart and hope to die, stick a needle in my eye.

Sonny whispers in Tricia's ear. Her eyes widen at the juiciness of the secret

A large crowd of boys bursts suddenly through them, screaming

The Boys Back of the bus! Back of the bus!

On hearing this, all the kids make a wild dash for the back of the bus

*

On the bus

The children are all on a level, popping up when they hear their name in the register. Everyone is talking throughout as Miss Sheehan speaks

Miss Sheehan Right, settle down. Rab? Stop. James! Enough. OK. Tricia — stop talking, please. Rab. That's enough. SHUT UP! Thank you. Right. Sonny?
Sonny Yes, Miss Sheehan.
Miss Sheehan Anna?
Anna Yes, Miss Sheehan.
Miss Sheehan James?

Pause

Tricia (*doing a "der-brain" impression*) James!
James What? Oh, yes, Miss.
Miss Sheehan What did you miss?
James What? Oh, yes, Miss Sheehan.
Miss Sheehan Miracle?
Miracle Yes, Miss Sheehan.
Miss Sheehan Jenelle?

Jenelle Arsenal beat Tottenham two-nil.
Miss Sheehan And what a game it was. Rab?
Rab Here, Miss Sheehan.
Miss Sheehan Sam?
Sam (*loudly*) Yes, Miss Sheehan!
Miss Sheehan Tricia?
Tricia (*even louder*) Yes, Miss Sheehan.

It is now apparent that this is a game. The one who can answer in the loudest voice wins

Miss Sheehan Chrissy?
Chrissy (*louder*) Here, Miss.
Miss Sheehan Stacey?
Stacey (*louder*) Yes, Miss!
Miss Sheehan Bee?
Bee (*almost screaming*) Yes, Miss!
Miss Sheehan Ben?
Ben (*normal volume*) I am present, Miss Sheehan.
Everyone (*doing elaborate "der-brain" impressions*) Mr Bean! Mr Bean!

Tom, a small boy, gets on the coach and looks for a space. Despite the abundance of free seats, they all appear to be saved

Rab (*on seeing Tom enter the coach*) Tramp! Incoming, lads.
James You're late, Tom. You Michael Jackson wannabe.

The register is still going on in the background

Tom attempts to sit down next to Matthew

Matthew Sorry saved.
Chrissy Sorry saved.
Stacey Sorry saved.

Many are still waving goodbye to their parents through the window, but are beginning to tire of this activity and are chatting to friends at the same time

Rab Sorry. This is a Clark's shoe-free zone.
Miss Sheehan Rab, let Tom sit there please.
Tom Thank you, Miss. (*He sits*)
Rab Miss, I'm charging you with the doctor's bill when we all catch Lurgi.

James (*to Rab*) Jexies!

Rab and James touch their heads, then cross their arms to touch their shoulders then touch their waists

Everyone Lurgis ejected for life!

Miss Sheehan OK, has everyone got their sick bags?

Everyone (*while holding up see-through plastic bags*) Yes, Miss.

Bee Can't we get the paper sort, Miss? These sort are disgustin'. If anyone's sick you can see right through them.

Stacey The paper ones are worse though. If you're sick in those, they go all soggy at the bottom and burst.

Bee Thanks for that, Stace.

Anna Oh. Miss. I've left my pack-lunch box in the classroom. Can I go and get it?

James No, you can starve.

Miss Sheehan Quickly.

Anna Thanks, Miss.

Anna leaves

The electronic sound of a DS becomes audible. It is traced to Chrissy. Everyone in the surrounding seats leans in, intent on seeing how badly she's doing

Sam (*doing a "der-brain" impression*) No! You've got to go down under that path and switch the lever, then you can get over the bridge. No! Only Puss-in-Boots can climb that wall!

Chrissy (*sarcastically*) You don't say.

Sam Jump! Jump! Ah. You missed it.

Stacey It ain't fair. I'm feelin' car sick.

Tom We haven't even set off yet.

Every time Tom speaks he is mocked

Ben By my calculation we should have left fifteen minutes ago ——

Rab Quiet everyone. He speaks. Mr Bean has something he wishes to share. What was it? Mr Bean?

Throughout this speech Rab is impersonating Ben behind his back

Ben According to my watch, the accuracy of which is governed by satellite, we should have begun our journey fifteen minutes, twelve seconds and ... thirty-two milliseconds ago ——

Everyone Shut up, Mr Bean!

The coach revs up, and from the movement of the children and the frantic waving out of the back window, it is obvious that their journey has begun

*

On three seats of the coach sit Tricia, Sonny and Jenelle. Tricia is still waving frantically out of the back window

Tricia Bye, Mum. Mummy ... (*She cries*) I'm homesick.
Jenelle Shaaaame! Tricia's crying!
Tricia I'm not cryin', I'm not. Anyway, don't vex me. You're not in the gang. Me and Sonny are a gang and we're well nang. We're the Nang Gang.

Sonny and Tricia do their elaborate handshake

Jenelle (*kissing her teeth*) You fink I wanna be in your neeky gang?
Tricia Yeah, well we've got gang secrets. We tell each other everything. Everything. You wouldn't believe some of the stuff Sonny's told me.

Tricia suddenly appears far more pally with Jenelle than with Sonny. Sonny looks left out. He grabs Tricia's arm

Jenelle Like what?
Sonny You say anything, I'll never speak to you ever again.
Jenelle What sort of secrets 'as he told you?
Tricia I'm sworn to secrecy.
Jenelle Yeah, obviously. What are they?
Sonny I'll break your neck!
Tricia Well. Don't say that I told you, but Sonny well fancies you.
Sonny (*suddenly sitting back in his seat*) That's not ... you said ... you weren't gonna ... anyway, it's not true anyway.
Tricia You love her.
Sonny I don't. In fact, I hate her, see? (*He pulls a disgusting face at Jenelle*)
Tricia (*singing*) Sonny and Jenelle up a tree. K-I-S-S-I-N-G!
Sonny Look! You're the most smelly (*mouthing*) bitch I ever saw. (*Proudly to Tricia*) See?
Tricia Hold hands! Hold hands!
Sonny I hate her! Look! (*He hits Jenelle*)
Jenelle OW!
Tricia You two are gonna get married.
Jenelle I don't fink so.

Sonny I'm never talkin' to you ever again.

Tricia Oh, Sonny. You're my best friend.

James (*popping up*) Oi, do you wanna hear the sickest thing ever?

Tricia James! This is an AB conversation. C your way out of it.

James (*making letter symbols with his fingers M W M*) Your Mum Works in McDonald's.

Tricia You think you're so nang.

James Yep.

Tricia Well, you're not. (*Shouting*) Hands up who thinks James is nang.

Rab shoots his hand up. After a glare from James, so does Sonny. Jenelle has her hand sort of half-way. James doesn't even look to see who's on his side

See? Three.

James No one else heard you. And anyway, I'm not gonna even ask anyone what they think of you, 'cos you'd be so upset that you'd throw yourself off the coach. And you're so fat that you'd go right through the world and come out at Australia.

Tricia No.

James You would.

Tricia Wouldn't.

James Would.

Ben Actually, she wouldn't.

Tricia Thanks, Mr Bean.

Ben Yes, even weighing nine hundred and fifty thousand, billion, zillion tonnes ...

Tricia (*hitting Ben*) Thanks a lot.

Ben No no. Just supposing. Well, even then, due to gravity, the furthest Tricia could possibly fall would be to the centre of the Earth.

Tricia Yeah. Well it's great down there. I've been.

James That's a lie.

Bee Yeah, what's it like then?

Tricia Well, you go down this tunnel in Staffordshire ...

Anna That's where we're going, isn't it?

Tricia Yeah, see, I'm not actually supposed to tell you this but we're not actually going to Alton Towers at all.

Anna What?

Tricia We are actually going to the centre of the Earth.

Bee (*sarcastically*) Yeah, right.

Bee, James, Anna, Ben try and shout Tricia down

Tricia No, it's true. Ask my granny. Ask my turtle. We're on a mission but we don't know it.
Everyone Eh?
Tricia At least you lot don't know it.
Everyone Eh?
Tricia What I'm gonna tell is very dangerous information.
Everyone Eh?
Tricia In fact, it's probably best that I don't tell.
Anna No, tell.
Tricia No, Anna. It's too dangerous for you to know.
Everyone (*disappointed*) Oo-oh.

*

Tricia So, you two. When's the wedding?
Jenelle Shut up. Anyway, Simon might get jealous.
Tricia Who's Simon?
Sonny The pieman.

Sarcastic laughs from Tricia and Jenelle, referring to Sonny's unsuccessful joke

Jenelle You bricked it, batty boy.
Tricia That's so sad. So who is Simon?
Jenelle He's my boyfriend. He's thirteen.
Tricia ⎱
Sonny ⎰ (*together*) THIRTEEN?!!
Sonny Older boys are stupid.
Jenelle Older boys are the best.
Tricia That's like your dad though!
Sonny They only want you for one thing.
Jenelle What do they want me for?
Sonny Well. They only want you for one thing. Like, that thing could be anything, but, thing is, they only want you for that and not for nothing else. My uncle's older than my aunt and she said that's true. I reckon it's her cooking.
Tricia She good?
Sonny Yeah, she made this bare yummy ice-cream cake for my eighth birthday. But she is fat. Like really really fat. She's one of those people you can't imagine on the loo.
Tricia Yeah, 'cos like if she sat on the loo, all her flab would bulge over the edges and touch the floor either side.
Jenelle Gross! You two are so immature.

Sonny Just 'cos you've got an older boyfriend.
Tricia I am eight-and-three-quarters and I am almost nine.
Jenelle I'm nine this week.
Tricia Well, I'm nine last week. I'm eleven. I'm fifteen. I'm seventeen.
I work in Sue Ryder. I'm married.
Jenelle Shut —
Tricia I am married.
Jenelle To who?
Sonny Michael Jackson.
Jenelle Urghh.
Tricia No. Robbie.
Jenelle What, so you're Mrs Williams?
Tricia Yeah.
Jenelle But you're not. Oh deeeee-aaaar. You got slewed!
Tricia I am.
Jenelle No. You're Tricia Park. Which means you lied. Liar, liar, pants
on fire.
Tricia No, but you see, 'cos you're not s'posed to get married until
you're grown-up, I have to have a fake name, 'cos I've got married
before I should and if the police found out they'd hang me.
Sonny Don't be stupid. They don't have the death penalty any more.
Tricia Yeah, they do. But only for treason and getting married to pop
stars when you're too young.
Sonny What's treason?
Tricia It's cussing down the Royal Family.
Jenelle Sonny, do you really think I'm buff?
Sonny Yeah!
Tricia (*very loudly*) Woah! Everyone! Sonny's telling Jenelle that he
loves her.
Everyone (*getting higher and higher pitched*) Oooooooooooooooooooo!
Sonny No I never.
Jenelle You said I was buff.
Sonny Exactly.
Tricia Sonny, do you actually know what "buff" means?
Sonny Yeah.

Sonny becomes aware that everyone is listening in

Tricia What, then?
Sonny (*suddenly unsure*) It's like a mixture between (*mouthing*) bitch
and guff.

Everyone does elaborate "der-brain" impressions. Sonny is mortified

*

James (*off*) Who let off a smelly one? Come on, own the stinker. Who ate egg this morning?
Chrissy Anyway, you fancy the driver.

Stacey looks at the driver then sticks her fingers down her throat

Stacey (*referring to the driver*) That's disgusting. He is butters. And he stinks of piss.
Chrissy Perfect match, then. You told me the other day that you wet the bed and that your mum got well angry with you.
Rab (*popping up*) Rah. She got yer. Boyage! (*Right in her face*) You got slewed!
James ⎫
Rab ⎬ (*together*) How-do-you feel?
James What happened?
Rab She wets the bed.
James Oh, tramp! You live in a cardboard box.
Stacey I didn't. That's not ... It wasn't me.
James It wasn't you? What, someone's been crawlin' into your bed at night, pissin' and then crawlin' out again?
Stacey I spilled a glass of water, all right?

Sarcastic, sympathetic nods, and chin scratching

Chrissy An' I feel sorry for your sister who has to sleep in the same bed.
James ⎫
Rab ⎬ (*together*) How-do-you feel?
Stacey That is a lie. My sister ... I haven't got a sister.
Chrissy Yes you do.
Stacey All right. But she doesn't sleep in the same bed. We've got bunk beds, and I get the top one 'cos I'm good.
Rab So it must drip through.
Chrissy Urrrgh.
Stacey I don't wet the bed. I don't wet the bed. I'm not listening. (*With her hands over her ears*) Din din din. I'm not listening.
Rab I wouldn't sleep with you.

Pause

I mean, in a bed.
Stacey I'm going to the toilet. (*She sticks two fingers up at Sonny. He does the same to her*)

Rab Yeah, we wouldn't want you doin' it on your seat.

James P'raps you should sleep on the bog. That would solve all your problems.

*

Ben The turbulence is interfering with my digestive tract. By the time we get there I'll be too sick to go on the any of the big rides.

Sam Have you been on the big one at Alton Towers?

Miracle The Corkscrew! I've been on that one! It's wicked, innit?

Sam Yeah, I've been on that, like, ten times. I love that bit, you know, when you're slowly goin' up and then ...

Tom Oh yeah, an' then you, like wait at the top for, like, ages ...

Sam It's only a couple of seconds ...

Tom Yeah, but it feels like ...

Sam Yeah, it feels like ages, and then suddenly it dips ...

Everyone screams

Sonny Yeah, an' your tummy gets left behind.

Sam Yeah, your tummy. An' then before you know it you're goin' ...

Both have begun to live the ride and, as their audience watches, they too begin to swerve and lurch with Rab and Louise

Miracle On the upside down bit ...

Tom An' you're "Waaaah!" and "Ooooo!"

Jenelle An' then you turn the corner an' ...

Miracle You think you're gonna come off the rails and "Weeeee!" and "Aaaaaargh!"

All screaming and shouting together

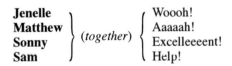

Jenelle		Woooh!
Matthew	*(together)*	Aaaaah!
Sonny		Excelleeeent!
Sam		Help!

Etc.

Ben And then it's the end of the ride.

Everyone Shut up, Mr Bean.

Miracle We haven't got to the best bit yet.

Matthew So you start to climb up again ...

Everyone is leaning back as they climb the second loop. Then they hang at the top and bomb down

Sonny An' now we're right upside down ...
Jenelle An' we stop for a couple of seconds ...
Sam Yeah, you stop right upside down ...

The children all appear to be hanging upside down. Suddenly there is a complete silence — a long pause while they hang

Miracle And then ...

Everyone lurches forward and hurtles down the second loop, a look of terror on their faces. They all scream and shout together

Sonny		Help!
Tom		I want to get off!
Sam	(*together*)	Wicked!
Sonny		Can I open my eyes yet?
Jenelle		I'm gonna die! I'm gonna die!
Matthew		I hate it! I hate it!

Miracle An' we're goin' round the corner ...

They lurch to the side as they go round a sharp bend

An' we're comin' to the end ...

They are all thrown forward as the ride stops. They pant heavily

What do you think?
Tom (*breathless*) That's excellent.

*

Stacey returns

Stacey (*to James*) Out.
James Talk about take yer time on the bog. That bog's for everyone, you know. Not just for people with pissing problems.
Stacey Get out of my seat.
James Urrrgh. Yours, is it? I thought it was a bit damp.
Stacey If you ain't careful I'll piss on you.

James Wow. You've been on the bog all that time and you've still got enough wee left to piss on me? You're amazing, Stace. I gotta say. You're world-class pisser of the year.

*

Anna Please tell me what's going on, Tricia.

Tricia (*super-fast*) Oh well, Sonny said Jenelle was buff, and I told them about how I'm married to Robbie, then someone guffed, then Stacey said she fancies the driver who smells of piss and then she wet her seat —

Anna No, the secret mission. The centre of the Earth.

Tricia Oh, that. (*Pause*) Well, I suppose if I tell you what's going on you might be more prepared. We're being kidnapped for ... a super top-secret, mega-scary mission. They're going to watch us to see if we can live down there.

Anna They?

Tricia (*whispering*) Terrorists.

Anna Terrorists?

Tricia Very dangerous people. They all look like Simon Cowell off *X Factor*. They're not really humans. They're robots. They're programmed to kill. They've all got these really dead eyes and really tight jeans which are pulled up suspiciously high. And they are completely bald, but have this like fake hair which is what is used to hide the guns what pop out of their heads. And they brainwash chidren by making them listen to bad music. Very dangerous. The X-Bots.

Anna }

Bee } (*together*) No!

Tricia It's an experiment. An evil plot.

Bee They wouldn't pick us. They'd want people who were properly trained.

Tricia No, that's the whole point. They've got to put down people who don't know anything about the experiment. People who aren't gonna grass them up — school children. It's obvious. People they can 'nipulate.

Anna You mean we're goin' down there for the rest of our lives?

Tricia Yeah. Why'd you think I got homesick at the beginning? D'you think I'd get homesick if I was just going to Alton Towers for the weekend? No, of course I wouldn't. But for the rest of my life ...

Anna But I didn't even say goodbye to my mum. I just told her not to forget to record *EastEnders*.

Tricia Ah, well. It's too late now. And you're gonna miss *EastEnders* for the rest of your life.

Bee Doesn't matter anyway. It's ending soon.

Anna Isn't there any way of stopping it?

Bee No, they're gonna blow up Albert Square and that'll be the end ——

Anna No, I mean going to the centre of the Earth.

Tricia 'Fraid not.

Anna Well, shouldn't we tell Miss Sheehan?

Tricia She's in on it. So's the coach driver. There's no hope, I'm afraid.

Anna Miss!

Tricia You could ask her. But she's gonna deny it, 'cos they're not gonna tell us until there's no way out. They can't take the risk.

Anna MISS!

Tricia Miss Sheehan's a terrorist. (*Pause*) She's trying to find out about the centre of the Earth for Bin Laden so they can burrow underneath and set up camp there and then spring up from the sewers when we're least expecting it and kill us all and take over the world.

Anna But Miss Sheehan always seemed so nice.

Tricia I know. I'm sorry you had to learn this way.

Bee (*to Tricia*) But wait a minute. Miss Sheehan supports Arsenal.

Tricia All part of the cunning disguise.

Anna How do you know all this?

Tricia Well, it makes sense, doesn't it?

Rab You've been watchin' way too many movies, Trish.

James Yeah, those "U"s that you've been watching 'ave gone straight to your head.

Rab Yeah, like *Tweenies' and the Teletubbies' Big Day Out*!

Rab and James do impressions of Tweenies and Teletubbies

Tom (*urgently*) I heard Mr Harris and Miss Sheehan talking ——

Rab Urggggh, Tom, don't come near me with those shoes!

James That's deep.

Rab No, listen, they went out when the dinosaurs came in!

James That's sad.

Rab Yeah, I know — but I just said it to keep in with Tom.

James Oh you're a joker, bruv. Oh dear, Tom.

Rab ⎫
James ⎭ (*together*) How-do-you-feel?

Rab Arrrgh. You gonna beat me up, Tom? No, Tom, please don't beat me up. I'll have to go and find Mumsy.

James Where does your mum shop, Tom? Oxfam?

Rab No, Ultra Oxfam! Tom. Did you know?

James Did you know? Did you know?

Rab That cats lay eggs. That's true actually, please.

Tom No they don't.
Rab Yes they do 'cos my dad told me actually.
James An' his dad's a scientist.
Rab Did you know that?
Tom Yeah.

Hysterical laughing

(*Desperately*) They don't lay eggs. I meant about his dad. They don't lay eggs. I meant I knew his dad's a scientist.
Rab Vexed. You got slewed.
James 'At was wicked. 'At was wicked.
Tom (*desperately*) They don't lay eggs. I know they don't.
Rab Aw, what a nice *Winnie the Pooh* lunch box, Tom. Was it part of the Oxfam summer sale? Ultra mega Oxfam summer sale? Ultra mega Oxfamopolis?
Tom Please listen! Please listen!
Bee Rab! Let him speak.
Rab Shup, Bee, his mum's a Teletubby.
Bee Let him speak.
Rab (*mimicking*) Let him speak.
Tom I heard him and Miss Sheehan talking.
Bee What were they saying?
Tom That the school journey might not go quite as planned, and that knowing us we'd all end up lost.
Tricia How did they look?
Tom I don't know. Kind of shifty.
Tricia Mmmm. They were talking in code.
Bee Mr Harris is one of them?
Tricia All the teachers are. Those meetings they have. They're all to plan how they're gonna capture us. It was Mr Harris's idea. He's a nasty piece of work is Harris. (*Whispering*) An X-Bot.
Miracle He does wear his trousers suspiciously high.
Tom And his hair is definitely fake.
Anna And in assembly when we're doing singing his eyes do look very dead.
Bee That is spooky.
Miracle But I still don't understand how come you know all about these terrorists.
Tricia Ah, well, my dear Miracle. That's a bit more cleverer. For a start, Sheehankov is a known terrorist name, but to fool us all she's cunningly missed off the "kov" bit. And also purple is the terrorist's

special colour code, and, as we all know, purple is Miss Sheehan or should I say Miss Sheehankov's favourite colour.

They look astounded at Miss Sheehan

Tom (*tentatively*) What does the purple code mean?
Tricia It means "kill the children". Depending on what colour they're wearing, the chiefs can tell what kind of terrorist department they work for.
Sam You can tell they're terrorists by the colour of their skin. Miss Sheehan isn't dark.
Miracle That's rubbish, Sam. Terrorists can have any colour skin. My mum says so. She says that the worst kind are the ones that pretend to be good people who have smiley families and nice suits and all that and are secretly selling people bombs.
Sam Yeah well, my mum said that if dark people weren't allowed to come into the country it would never have happened.
Miracle Yeah but everyone knows your mum's a racialist.
Sam No, she's not. She just says we got enough of them now.
Miracle That is so wrong, Sam. If I tell Miss Sheehan that you're a racialist you'll be in big trouble. Miss!
Sam No, don't! Miss Sheehan's a terrorist.
Tom But I thought terrorists live in cyberspace.
Tricia Yeah and where do you think cyberspace is?
Everyone Where?

Tricia points down, all look down

Tricia The terrorists are just a front ——
Everyone For what?

Pause

Tricia That ain't the point. Point is we're on a school journey to the centre of the Earth.
Rab (*popping up*) Cack. Cack. The liar needs a slap.
Sam (*spotting a Mini out the window*) Mini Cooper! No returns. (*He punches Stacey*)
Stacey (*punching him back*) Mini Cooper!
Sam Oi, you can't do that. I said no returns.
Stacey No you never.
Anna Yeah he did, Stacey.
Sonny Umm. You get a free slap for that, Sam.

Stacey No! That ain't fair.

Rab It's the law, Stace. We can't make exceptions, can we Sonny?

Sonny No. Put out your hand, Stace.

Stacey No! Please don't!

Everyone (*getting higher and higher pitched*) Oooooooooooooooo!

Sam slaps Stacey's hand, hard. She bursts into tears

James Shut up, Stacey. You better be tougher than that when the terrorists come for us.

Hal (*popping up*) What's this?

Bee Trish reckons we're goin' to the centre of the Earth, wiv purple spies or something.

Sonny Oh yeah, I wonder what the Arabesques are a front for?

Ben (*popping up*) You're getting it all muddled. The Arab culture is ancient and fascinating ——

Rab
Jenelle
Anna ⎫ Shut up, Mr Bean!
James ⎭

Ben They invented the alphabet ——

Everyone Shut up, Mr Bean!

Jenelle Nah, he's right. It's not the Arabesques. It's the Funny Mentalists.

Stacey It's the North Koreans what are really behind it all.

Tricia Ahh, Stacey. I would never have guessed.

Stacey Guessed what?

Tricia That it was you. I was told someone would be sent to give me vital information. Thank you.

Stacey (*confused, but pleased with the attention*) Oh that's all right, I mean think nothing of it ... comrade.

Jenelle Right, so let's look at the facts.

Tom There are no facts. Only guesses.

Tricia You shut up. How old are you?

Tom (*smugly*) Ten in three weeks. How old are you?

Tricia Yeah, well that don't matter. A few months don't make no difference to anyone. Anyway, Clever-Arse — where do you think all the terrorists are hiding and making the MWD?

Tom It is too hot for anything to live down there. Science says so.

Tricia I don't know what scientists you've been chattin' with, batty boy, but the one I've spoken to lives down there. So, so much for all your "science says so" crap.

She sticks her tongue out at Tom

Rab Murked boy. That was jokes, Trish. Pity you were talkin' outta your little brown star.

Everyone laughs at Tricia. Rab and James slap hands

Tricia Fine. When you get down there you'll be sorry. You'll wish you listened to your dear old mate Trish when you're trapped by evil terrorists, poking you with needles and pulling your hair out and ...

*

Rab Who's seen *War of the Worlds*?
Miracle Yeah. It's bare good!
James I thought it was crap.
Miracle Yeah, I s'pose it wasn't that good.
Rab What's your favourite bit?
Miracle Oh, urm ... I saw it ages ago so ... urm I can't really remember.
James It's only just come out.
Miracle (*desperately*) Oh. Maybe I'm getting it muddled up with another film ...
Rab Which other film?
Miracle I don't know what it's called. I saw it ages ago.
James So you haven't actually seen *War of the Worlds*?
Miracle Urm ... No. I don't think I have. I got muddled.
Rab Do you like the bit when the aliens come?
Miracle I told you. I haven't seen it.
Rab No, but that bit's on the trailer. You must've seen it on TV.
Miracle Oh, yeah. Course. (*Quickly changing the subject*) So Trish, tell us more about the terrorists.

*

Stacey How do you get down to the centre of the Earth? I mean, how would you, supposin' we was goin', which I don't believe anyway.
Tricia Ah, well. That's the cunning bit.
James Whoever nicked my Twix had best give it back unless they wanna die a slow and painful death.
Jenelle Vex up! Stress monkey! Watch it, everyone. James might turn nasty.
Tricia You know the rollercoaster at Alton Towers?
Miracle Yeah. The Corkscrew.
Rab Yeah, it's wicked, man.
Jenelle Yeah, that bit when it dips down is blindin'.

Everyone does rollercoaster noises

Chrissy Yeah and then you start goin' up slowly ...
Rab And then you get to the top bit ...

They are all set to take another ride on their imaginary rollercoaster

Tricia No, not that one. You know the one in the dark? The underground one?
Chrissy Oh, The Blackhole?

They all get ready to go down The Blackhole

Tricia Yeah, whatever. Miss Sheehankov will give ——
Matthew Sheehankov?
Jenelle It's Miss Sheehan's secret Funny Mentalist name.
Matthew Oh, right.
Tricia Yeah, well she'll give the signal when the train's filled up with us lot, and the man what works The Blackhole will switch the tracks so instead of goin' back to the beginning, the ground opens up and we go plummeting down into the centre of the Earth.

They all go down The Blackhole

James Rah, that's sick man.
Miracle Yeah, like the longest rollercoaster ever ... straight down ...
James Mad.
Tom Wow. Those terrorists are clever.
Jenelle Yeah.
Anna But our parents will notice we've gone.
Tricia For a while, yeah. But you know all these kids that vanish like when they're skiing and stuff?
Miracle Yeah?
Tricia That's where they've gone. We'll probably see them down there.
Matthew They died, didn't they?
Tricia That's what everyone was told. But it's all part of The Spirisy.
Anna The Spirisy?
Tricia That's what it is. The Spirisy.
Anna What's The Spirisy?
Tricia You know, like Diana.
Chrissy Who's Diana?
Tricia You know, the princess who was killed by the Queen. That was the beginning of The Spirisy. The Queen wanted Diana to marry her

son but Diana wanted to marry Saddam Bin Laden so the Queen poisoned Diana's driver ——

Matthew Oh is that why he knocked down the Twin Towers?

Tricia Yes, because Diana had twins in her tummy when she was killed by the Queen, so Saddam knocked down the Twin Towers to get revenge, then Prime Minister Bush smashed up the Arabists, because he's in love with the Queen, who's actually a lizard. Now Saint Obama is trying to put it all right, but Prince Harry is going to turn into a lizard like his granny (that's what he was trying to do in that hotel room) and lead the Arabist Spring — where they all spring up out of the centre of the Earth when we least expect it.

Chrissy Oh no, not Harry. I well fancy him.

Everyone Oooooooooooooo!

Sonny Oh is this spirisy thing something to do with the Nasties?

Tricia Be careful, Sonny. You're closer to the truth than you know.

James The Nasties?

Sonny You know the ones who burned loads of people in chimneys and gave out gold stars.

James Oh yeah, they're cool.

Ben You know there is a theory that the Nazis ——

Everyone Shut up Mr Bean!

Sonny No, I want to hear this.

Ben There is a theory that the Nazis were simply one incarnation of a much more ancient and secretive cult, that has emerged throughout the ages to perform genocides.

Rab What is he talkin' about?

Ben Apparently a large amount of energy is released during mass murder and if you know the technique you can absorb it and become instantly immortal. That's what the Nazis were trying to do ...

Sonny What, so the Nasties never actually went away? We never actually beat them at war?

Tricia No, they just went underground.

James What, so the Nasties are running The Spirisy from under the ground?

Tricia What have I been trying to tell you?

Bee But how did these skiing dead kids get down?

Tricia Similar way to the rollercoaster. Only the chair-lift things suddenly change course and go down.

Miracle So what they gonna say happened to us?

Tricia Oh, we'll probably be one of those "School Bus Off Cliff" tragedies.

Rab You talk the biggest pile of cack ever.

Shouts of agreement

Tricia No, but no, shut up, right, no shut up, listen right. I know it sounds stupid but I mean, it sounded stupid to me when I first heard it from the head of the British Intelligence ...

Tom You said you put two and two together.

Tricia Ah, well, my dear Tom. I'm afraid it's a bit more complicated than that. I am in fact a spy. Working under cover. Posing as just an ordinary schoolgirl, when actually I am Britain's last hope at exposing The Spirisy. I shouldn't be telling you this. I could be putting you all in mortal danger.

Pause

James No. (*Pause*) Carry on.

Tricia No. I mustn't. If the Nasties found out that you knew they'd probably murder you. Pull your heads off with this special new machine that — like — pulls your heads off. It like sort of twists it a bit ...

James I'm gonna be a Torture and Killing Machine designer when I'm older. I'm gonna design things like what you've never heard of. That like has little stabbing little pins and sucks the jelly bit in your eyes out so they shrivel up and fall out and like cuts this hole in your tummy and pulls out your guts and plucks your hairs out one by one, and, for like, old men, it would do your nostril hairs as well ——

Tom Yeah, but ——

James No. Quiet. I'm talking. It pulls your fingers out and sticks sharp points up your nostrils that makes it bleed everywhere and it pierces your brain, and it's red hot — no, white hot, so it frazzles your brain but you don't die yet because your brain's not completely burned yet, and you can still feel pain. And sharp knives dig under your fingernails ——

Rab Is that before or after they've been pulled out?

James Shut up! (*His eyes widen — a terrifying glare*) Before. And then, when your brain's burned out completely, and your eyes have fallen out, and your fingers have been pulled out, then this claw will come out and it will chicken-scratch your heart until you're dead. (*He rubs his hands and grins*)

Shocked faces

Rab (*sarcastically*) Nice job.

James Or I might be a doctor.

Pause

Ben You could be both. (*Pause*) Being a doctor would give you access to people to test your equipment on.

James (*seeing it. Dreamily*) A sick doctor ...!

Tricia Has this got anything to do with what I was sayin' ?

James You was talkin' about the Nasties' Killing Machine.

Tricia Yeah, but that doesn't mean that you can just go raving on like something out of Amityville. So shut it.

James Yeah, well someone nicked my Twix. I was annoyed, innit?

Tricia You're such a weirdo.

Ben Don't, Tricia. His sadistic tendencies may be useful to us when we get to the centre of the Earth.

Tricia Yeah, whatever.

*

Chrissy You ever been to a funeral?

Bee Yeah.

Chrissy I've been to two funerals

Bee Yeah, I go to funerals every single Monday.

Chrissy Yeah, what happens, then?

Bee They bury people, don't they.

Chrissy Yeah, but ——

Bee An' I go to bonfires as well. That's when they put someone in the bonfire and watch them die slowly — and then laugh. And then they get all the ashes and make the relatives eat it.

Sam Doesn't it taste 'orrible though?

Bee It tastes of them. Like, if I were to take a bite out of you now, I'd taste you and remember that taste, right, and then if someone burnt loads of people and put all their ashes in bowls, I could taste each one and see which one was you.

Sam Really?

Bee Yeah.

Sam Shall we try it?

Bee Ain't touchin' you.

Sam I don't mean me.

Pause

Bee ⎫
Sam ⎬ Sonneeeee?
Chrissy ⎭

Sonny Yeah?

Bee Would you mind if we — urm — if we took a bite out of your leg and then burnt you with loads of other people and then tried you with a small spoon?

Sonny (*after a moment's thought*) Go on then.

Bee You go first.

Sam It was your idea.

Bee No, I've done it so often.

Sam Well, I don't want to lose my appetite. And anyway, they don't burn people.

Bee They do. It's called cremations. Sometimes they give you the ashes to take home in pots, other times people leave it there, and it gets given to cannibal countries. They prefer it to Nescafé.

Tom Cup-a-soup for cannibals. (*Pause*) My dad's friend who's a farmer ——

Sam Your dad's friend's not a farmer.

Tom He is.

Sam You dad hasn't got any friends.

Tom He has.

Sam You haven't got a dad.

Tom I have! Like I was sayin' right, my dad's friend who's a farmer ——

Sam Get on with it.

Tom He got caught under a tractor.

James (*without sympathy*) Did he die? Did he?

Tom No. He was all right.

James Yeah? Which bit of him got mashed?

Tom His legs. He ain't got no legs no more.

Bee What happened to his legs?

Tom They got caught under the tractor, didn't they?

Bee Yeah, but where are they now?

Tom They probably buried them.

Sam Yeah, you go to funerals. Ain't you ever seen legs buried?

Bee No, they only bury whole bodies where I go.

James I've just had an idea.

Sam What?

James Wouldn't it be cheaper to bury all your bits, like, separate, than buryin' them altogether. And also you'd get to have loads of funerals, like, one for your leg and one for your head. And you could go to your own funeral. Not your head's funeral obviously — or your heart's. But you could probably bury a leg or two before you died of blood loss. And ——

Sam It wouldn't be cheaper because you'd have to buy loads of different sized coffins. And they'd all have to be made specially to order, 'cos they don't normally make them different sizes to just ordinary people.

James Yeah. Some rich people get coffins for their cats and dogs. I'd need two dog ones, one for each leg, and two cat ones for my arms. And a small sheep one for my middle bit.

Matthew Buryin' bits separate would be a good idea to find out who really cared about you. It'd be a good idea for my mum 'cos she's always pretendin' to suicide herself to see if we care ...

Sam And do you?

Matthew We pretend we do. (*With pride*) If you've got a mad mum like me, you have to have a man from the council round every week to check on you.

Sam (*impressed*) Wow.

Chrissy Oh yeah I get that too, since my dad went to prison.

Sam What's your dad in prison for?

Chrissy Oh lots of stuff. (*Pause*) Mainly 'cos he killed this man.

James Rah! That's so cool.

Sam How did he do it? How did he do it?

Chrissy (*nonchalant*) Strangled him with his bare hands.

Tom Cor. I wish my dad was cool.

*

Anna What's it like down there, Tricia?

Tricia Down there? On the floor of the coach? I dunno. It's sort of ——

Anna No, the centre of the Earth. Will there be any lights? I can't go to sleep without a light on.

Tricia Well, yeah. Of course the Nasties are gonna make sure that there's some light otherwise they won't be able to see us through the video cameras to watch how we live.

Anna So there will be some light?

Tricia Yeah. There will be light. But wouldn't you rather live a life of darkness than know that you're being watched day after day, night after night?

Anna Er ... well, no. You see I can't go to sleep without a light.

Tricia Oh yeah. You said.

*

Stacey (*to James*) I don't think Miracle's got a TV.

Chrissy
Bee } What?

Stacey All that rubbish about *War of the Worlds*. I reckon she hasn't got one.

Chrissy Yeah and she reckoned that some boy band was on *X Factor*! That's what she said. BOY BAND!

Stacey ⎫
Bee   ⎬ (*amazed*) No!

Bee (*leaning in to the conversation*) When I went to her house she said it was at the mender's.

Stacey How long ago was this?

Bee About three months ago.

James She ain't got a TV? Oi, Rab. Get this. Miracle ain't got a telly!

Rab Rah! Miracle! Are you a tramp or what? (*In front of the whole coach*) Ain't you got a telly?

Everyone laughs

Miracle What?

James You ain't got a telly!

Miracle Of course I do.

James Oo yeah.

Miracle I do.

Rab All right then. How does the Muller advert go then?

Miracle Isn't that the one when ... there's the mum at the breakfast ——

Everyone NO! Five-six-seven-eight. (*They all sing Nina Simone's "Ain't Got No — I Got Life" from the Müller advert*)

Rab Lead a Muller Life!

Everyone T-E-L-L-Y-T-E-L-L-Y-T-E-L-L-Y You ain't got a telly!

The chant gets faster and faster and more and more in Miracle's face

All repeat until Miracle breaks down

Miracle (*through terrible sobs*) You don't know what it's like. My mum won't let me have one. She says it rots your brain. She makes me do stuff in the garden and draw and read and play the saxophone instead. She's so horrible. She's like a witch. I hate her so much.

Tricia Miracle, don't worry. It's not that bad. (*Pause, then declaring loudly*) I haven't got one either.

Miracle Really?

James (*to Tricia*) Urggh you filthy tramp. Get back in your cardboard box.

Everyone starts teasing Tricia

Jenelle Oh my God! Shut up! Can anyone else hear that ticking?

The paranoia builds up as they search for the source of the ticking, finally traced to ... Rab

Rab Booom!

Screams

Jenelle That is not even funny, Rab. Now that we know Miss Sheehankov is a terrorist you shouldn't make jokes like that ...
Sam Jenelle, don't worry. They need us to be alive ... so they can watch us, right, Trish?
Tom Brainwash us, more like.
Rab (*popping up*) Shut up, Tom. Loser!
Tricia No, Rab. He's right. I didn't want to say this. But the experiment isn't to watch us. The experiment is to brainwash us. To turn us into Nasties.
Jenelle Why?
Tricia So that we will end up like Miss Sheehankov. Pretending to be a nice teacher what supports Arsenal so that we can capture more kids to brainwash. It's a vikkious [*sic*] cycle.
Miracle What are we gonna do, Trish?
Tricia We'll make a break for it when we're down there and hide out in this cave I know about that the terrorists don't know and keep guard ...
Jenelle Will we have someone on guard all night for the Nasties?
Tricia Er ... Yeah.
Jenelle Do I have to do it, Tricia? I don't think girls should have to do it.
Tricia No, sorry. Everyone has to do it.
James (*popping up*) I'll do it. It'll be like *Tomb Raider*. (*He mimes shooting up Nasties with deadly precision*). Mega death. (*He mimes a gore and blood splatter-fest*)
Jenelle Can I be partners with you, James? I think I'll feel safest with you.
James (*suddenly shy and coy*) Yeah, all right. If you like.
Sonny Jenelle? Don't you want to be partners with me?

Pause

*

Rab's face is wedged between Anna's and Tricia's two seats throughout the following

Anna Tricia, I've been doing some serious thinking. We've got to try and take control of this situation. We can't let them put us on that

rollercoaster. I can't live in the centre of the Earth. I have some tictacs
— I mean tactics.

Tricia You? You're scared of the dark!

Anna Well it's time for me to grow up.

Rab Waaaah! I can't believe that you think all this cack is actually true!

Anna It could be true. It could be true. We don't know. Nobody knows.

Everyone is now listening

We know that terrorists want to kill us and that they live in caves. We
know that Harris and Sheehankov were talking in code. We know that
purple is the terrorist code to "kill the children" ——

Jenelle — and that the Funny Mentalists are doing bombings ——

Sonny — and that the Nasties were never actually killed and are running
the whole spirisy ——

Stacey — and that behind them is the North Koreans ——

James — and that they have to brainwash us to turn us into terrorists ——

Anna Yeah. And Tricia heard it from the head of the British Intelligence.
If you can't trust the head of the British Intelligence then who can you
trust?

Miracle Exactly.

Tom But who's behind the North Koreans?

Miracle Let's ask Tricia.

Stacey Tricia, who's behind the North Koreans?

Tricia The most terrifying creature you can imagine. Like a jellyfish
octopus brain thing with tentacles and massive sharp long teeth. The
size of ... London. It lives right at the very centre of the Earth and its
tentacles reach all the way through the caves and networks that the
Nasties have built and instead of suckers there are cameras all over
his tentacles which are watching everyone all the time to see how the
brainwashing is going.

Rab (*suspiciously*) What's it called?

Tricia It's called a ... (*pronouncing it gruesomely*) Wikileaks!

Gasps

Tricia Because it's wicked. And it leaks poisonous goo.

Rab So that's who Wikileaks is! Oh my days — it is true!

Ben I think it is true.

James He speaks ——

Miracle Shut up, James. Let him have his say.

Rab Shup. You ain't got a telly.

Miracle What d'you think's true, Mr Bean?

Ben I think it is very possible that the terrorists could actually be living in the centre of the Earth. Tricia's accounts have in fact been most accurate.

Rab Tricia's whats have been what?

Tricia How would you know? I mean, they have been, but how the hell do you know that?

Ben (*after a pause*) I've been there.

Tricia Shut up.

Anna How did you get down?

Ben In a chairlift. Like Tricia said.

Tricia You can't of done.

Anna Is there any light?

Tricia I've already told you that there is.

Anna Well, yes, but, I mean, Ben's actually been there, so he's more likely to know for sure, isn't he?

Ben Don't worry, Anna. There is some light. Things produce their own natural light. Like glow-worms.

Anna Oh, good.

Tricia He doesn't know what he's talkin' about.

Chrissy He's been there. You've only heard about it from the British Intelligence.

Tricia I have been there.

Ben Oh? What is it like then?

Tricia Well, the area I went to, known as ... urm ... Lower Beemsbry, was made up of these huge caves. Dark, 'cept for when the light from the glow-worms shone on the bits of jewels in the walls. Lower Beemsbry is like the capital — 'cos it's the most beautiful area. There were dark passages everywhere, like corridors, leading off into different rooms. The floor's soft and sandy — it's actually jewel dust — so it sparkles. When I came back I still had some jewel dust on my shoes ——

Rab Let's see.

Tricia It's rubbed off now, stupid. Anyway, there are glow-worms, like Ben said. And glow-maggots. And the Nasties have glow-eels. I slept in one of the small caves — I had a huge, flat rock as a bedside table. I was only there for two days.

Everyone looks at Ben for a confirmation

Anna Ben?

Ben It's nothing like that. And there's no glow-eels.

Rab Mmmm. Nice imagination, Trish.

Tom It's too hot down there.

Ben Not if you wear this stuff called Starlite that a hairdresser in Manchester invented. A suit of Starlite, you could sit on the sun and be OK — on the surface only, obviously. No one believed this hairdresser. The Starlite was mouldable like plastic and yet virtually completely heatproof. Impossible, scientists said. But they tested it, and the laser they tested it with — which burns through slabs of iron in a millisecond — broke due to the reflection of heat. It was on television, but it was on BBC Two so none of you will have watched it. Hairdresser. In Manchester.

Pause. Ben looks at his audience through his extra-strong lens glasses and sucks meditatively on his pencil

Anna (*who appears to have been thinking hard*) Miss! Miss! Is Alton Towers near Manchester?
Miss Sheehan (*off*) Yes, not far!

The children look at each other for a tense moment

Jenelle Wow.
Tricia Mr Bean's lying.
Anna Ben is not lying.
Tricia He is. I'm the spy. I know what's going on. Ben's just makin' it up. He's never been there.
Ben Unlike you, I'm not one to boast about my part in such a serious affair as this.
Tricia Just 'cos you can say lots of stupid words that don't mean anything to anyone, you think you're really cool.
Anna What do we sleep on?
Ben Erm ... Oh, well when I was there we slept on ... erm ... rocks ...
Miracle How uncomfortable. Was it really bad?
Tricia Don't be ridiculous. They're trying to brainwash you into being like them. And I bet you they won't be sleeping on rocks.
Ben That's what I was about to say. I went before the terrorists had set up this experiment. (*Pause*) I was the first ever person there.
Tricia The brainwashing laboratory was set up in nineteen thirty-six. November. That's before you were born.
Ben Ah, yes. But the West side of the centre of the Earth. Not the bit that everyone goes to. (*Pause*) If you know so much about all this, tell me the name of the North Korean terrorist spy who is in charge.
Tricia Radkot Flipscoddle.
Miracle That doesn't sound North Korean.

Tricia Obviously. It's a codename. (*Pause*) All right then, what's his real name?

Ben hesitates for a moment

Tricia You don't know.

Ben No, I'm just wondering whether it's wise to tell you. (*Pause*) How do I know you are really who you say you are?

Tricia Oh this is stupid. I know you're lying. You know you're lying. So why bother?

Anna You just wanna have all the attention, Tricia. You just wanna be the one who knows it all. And you can't stand it when someone knows more than you, can you?

Tricia (*shouting*) It's got nothing to do with that! I know he's lying.

Stacey So he's lying and you're not? Is that it? Everything you say goes. Everything he says is cack? Is that it?

Tricia No, that's not it.

Chrissy Well, that's certainly what it seems like, Tricia.

Tricia Piss off, Chrissy. This has got nothin' to do with you.

Anna This has got everything to do with Chrissy and everyone else in class 4S. It's all of us that have gotta face this.

Matthew Maybe it's the time for the revolution!

Stacey What's that?

Matthew It's something they do the whole time in history. My mum's always on about it.

Rab Yeah but your mum's a loonytune.

Matthew Only 'cos the revolution hasn't come yet.

Stacey Well how do you do one?

Matthew You just, like, stop doing what anyone tells you. And throw stones and stuff. And like, demand your rights ——

Chrissy What's our rights?

James Not to be kidnapped by evil terrorists what are pretending to be nice teachers for a start ——

Sam Rah man, I totally believed that she supported Arsenal, you know ——

Tricia (*shouting*) Will you all just shut up and listen to me? I know that Ben is lying because ... because I made it up.

Rab What, about Sheehankov supporting Arsenal?

Tricia No. About going to the centre of the Earth.

Long silence

Anna Tricia, we all know you're tryin' to protect us from findin' out too much for our own safety — and it's very good of you — but now I think it's time that we all faced facts. Don't you?

Long pause

Tricia Yes. It's time. You're right. And it was for your protection. I
should of known I couldn't fool you lot.

*

Anna So, Mr Bean. Are you a spy?
Ben Well, as a matter of fact ... (*pause*) ... yes, I am.

*As everyone crowds around Ben, Tricia sulks in the background. Her
arms are folded, and whenever Ben says something she shakes her head
scornfully*

Stacey Surely you shouldn't say that in case one of us is a terrorist spy.
Ben Yes. (*Pause*) And I have my suspicions.

He nods towards the unaware Tricia

Stacey (*whispering*) Tricia?
Anna
Stacey } (*together*) No.
Ben (*leaning in to his eager listeners*) The name she gave of the terrorist
leader?
Anna
Stacey } (*together*) Yes?
Ben She said it was the codename?
Anna
Stacey } (*together*) Yes?
Ben The British don't know that codename. It's something we've been
trying to discover for years.
Stacey Then how come she knows it?
Ben I wonder.
Anna If it is true, then she'll try and warn Sheehankov. Try and tell her
that we know.
Stacey How long till we're there?
Ben (*looking at his watch*) Taking account of the late departure ...
Twelve minutes, seventeen seconds and ... twenty-six miliseconds.
Anna Twelve minutes. We have no time to lose.

*

*Rab and James can be heard screeching with laughter from behind the
seats*

James Look! Look! (*He produces one of the see-through sick-bags which appears to be full of vomit*)
Rab (*leaning over and pretending to be violently sick into the bag*) I've been sick! (*He passes the bag around for closer inspection*)
Bee I'm gonna make one too. (*She rummages around in her packed lunch, looking for things with which to concoct another bag of sick*)
Jenelle I'm actually gonna be sick. Miss! I'm gonna be sick!

Bee and Rab waft the fake sick in Jenelle's face, while making sick noises

Miss Sheehan The next one of you to do that will have to eat it.
Everyone Urghh.
Tricia Yeah. But it's all mashed up.
Jenelle I'm not jokin'. I'm gonna be sick. Get me a sick bag — quick!
Miracle They're all filled with mashed up pack lunch!
Jenelle Just get me anything! Quick!
Anna Here's one. (*She hands Jenelle one of the see-through sick-bags*)

Jenelle attempts to open the bag, but it's one of those plastic ones that stick together and you can't tell which end is which

Anna (*desperately*) I can't get it open!

Eventually Jenelle manages to open it, and is sick — much to everyone's enjoyment

Rab Look! Look! She 'ad egg for breakfast. She was the one who guffed!
James Oi leave her alone.
Everyone Oooooooooo!
Rab Excuse me, Miss. But Jenelle's just done exactly what you told us not to. She's put all her pack lunch — all mashed up — into a sick bag!
Chrissy Miss said the next one would have to eat it.
Rab (*triumphantly*) I know.
Bee That is pure jokes!
Sonny }
James } (*together*) Leave her alone!

They glare at each other

Miracle (*warning*) Sheehankov's coming!
Miss Sheehan Jenelle, did you do what I told you not to?

Jenelle No, it's really sick, Miss.
Chrissy Rab was tryin' to get Jenelle into trouble.
Miss Sheehan Well then Rab can eat it.
Rab No, Miss!

Everyone bursts out laughing and pushes the bag of sick towards Rab

No! Please, Miss. That's not funny. It's not even my sick! — I don't
like egg! Please, Miss. I was jokin'. Please, Miss, don't make me,
Miss! (*Almost in tears*) I'm sorry.
Miss Sheehan All right, that's enough.

Everyone reluctantly withdraws from Rab

Rab Thanks, Miss Sheehankov — urm Sheehan. Sorry, I meant Sheehan.

Everyone is glaring at Rab when he turns back to face them

I slipped.
Tom You slipped? You slipped? You idiot! You fool. Now Miss
Sheehankov knows that we know. There's no chance of escape now!
Miracle Look! Look! She's talking to the coach driver. She's telling
him that we know.
Tom There's no hope. You idiot!
Anna We should make plans.
Rab I'm really sorry.
Tom OK. Apology accepted. Now, come on. Let's decide what we're
gonna do.

Jenelle suddenly bursts into tears

Jenelle I'm scared.
Sonny (*putting his arm around her*) Don't worry, Jenelle. It's all gonna
be fine.
Anna Jenelle. Keep it down. If Sheehankov hears you she'll be over
here like a shot.
Miracle (*hissing*) She's coming!

Everyone sits back in their seats suddenly

James (*smiling sweetly*) Hello, Miss.
Miss Sheehan Are you all right, Jenelle? Do you want to come and sit
at the front for a bit?

Jenelle shakes her head, scared stiff

Sonny I'm looking after her, Miss. She's safe with me.
Miss Sheehan So Anna, what are you going to go on when we finally get there?

Anna stares up at her, terrified

What about the waterslide?
Anna Yes. The waterslide is fun.
Miss Sheehan And The Blackhole? I guess everyone will be going on that.
Anna (*catching eyes with Ben; quietly*) Yeah ... I don't think I will be going on The Blackhole ... Miss.
Miss Sheehan Oh, I'm sure you will, Anna. I'm going to make it my personal duty to get you all on that rollercoaster. Seeing you all screaming your little heads off will make the whole trip worthwhile.
Anna Oh, right. See you later, Miss.

All look at each other. Miss Sheehan returns to her seat

Miracle She knows.
Rab (*to Anna*) What's the plan?
 Anna We are going to have to get control of the coach.
Ben Five minutes, fifty-two seconds, twelve milliseconds.
Anna Is everyone in agreement?

Solemn nods

Tricia Don't be stupid. We can't do that. We're only kids. Can anyone drive? I mean, it's stupid. It's impossible. We are just gonna stay calm and see how it goes.

Ben looks at Anna as if to say "see?"

Anna Tricia. I'm beginning to wonder whose side you're on. First you tell us you're a British spy with nerves of iron ——
Tricia I didn't say nothin' about any iron ——
Anna — and now it seems that you're a terrorist, helping the Nasties to capture us.
Chrissy (*suddenly lashing out at Tricia, hysterical*) You filthy terrorist spy! You traitor! I can't believe I invited you to my birthday party! There's gonna be no traitors at my birthday party!

Chrissy breaks down in sobs

Tricia Chrissy! I'm not a terrorist spy. I'm not any sort of spy!
Ben As I suspected.
Tricia (*almost screaming*) Shut up! You're the evil one! You deserve
  to die!

Anna grabs hold of Tricia by the shoulders

Anna Shut up! You're hysterical! Sheehankov will be here any moment.
  Now, everyone just stay calm. Jenelle, do you need another sick bag?

Jenelle nods

Sonny ⎫
James ⎭ (*together*) I'll get one!

Sonny and James tussle over the sick bag. Sonny wins eventually

Miss Sheehan (*off*) What's going on back there?
Everyone Nothin' Miss.
Sonny A sick bag, Jenelle!
Jenelle Thank you Sonny. (*She is violently sick*)
Anna Now, we need to decide who's in charge of what.
James Rab an' me'll be in charge of the battle tactics.
Rab Now, has everyone got weapons?
Tom Oh yeah. I'll just get my Kalashnikov out of my backpack. You
  fool. Course we haven't got weapons.
Miracle What do we need 'em for, anyway?
Sam This thing has gotta be done using surprise tactics and weapons.
Jenelle Well, none of us got any knives or nothin' so what d'you
  suggest?
Matthew Pack lunch boxes? I mean, anything that will hurt if it hits
  you.
Miracle Satsumas. My mum packed five. Vitamin C.

Miracle passes the satsumas around

Anna Right, Tom, I'm making you Head of Communications.
Rab But he's a der-brain.
Anna Rab — it's time to pull together now. We can't afford to be
  fighting with each other.

Rab has to agree and he and Tom hug manfully

Anna Right 4S. Are you with me?
Everyone Sir, yes sir!
Anna I didn't hear you ——
Everyone Sir, yes sir!
Anna So, James, Rab. How do you suggest we take over the coach?
James Rab an' me'll crawl to the front of the coach an' get ready behind the driver.
Tom Chrissy should go too — her dad's a killer.
Rab Affirmative. Then you lot, after countin' to ten ——
Sam Silently.
James Yeah, obviously. Anyway ——
Tom If we all suddenly go silent they'll know something's going on.
Miracle Go on, James.
Anna No, Tom is Head of Communications and he's right. It needs to be better planned.
Miracle How long have we got?
Ben Two minutes, twenty-one seconds, forty milliseconds.
Anna Tom, what do you think?
Tom I think it would be better, if we sing a song and then arrange a certain point ——
James Yeah, whatever. Anyway, when you get to this certain point, we'll all charge to the front and attack Sheehankov ——
Tricia NO!
Anna Is there a problem with this plan?
Tricia Yes. What if Miss Sheehankov — I mean Miss Sheehan — isn't a terrorist after all?
Miracle If she's not a terrorist then why's she taking us to the centre of the Earth?
Tricia Maybe she's not.
Tom Forty-two seconds. What are we gonna sing?
Miracle (*to Tricia*) Why d'you think that?
Tricia I made it all up.

Miracle looks at the crowd of excited children and then back to Tricia

Miracle Why?
Jenelle What about Crazy Frog?
Tricia (*to Miracle*) I s'pose to make you all like me.
Tom Three times through.

Pause

Miracle Do you really not have a telly?
Tricia No, I do. I just said that so they'd stop picking on you.
Miracle That's the nicest thing anyone's ever done for me.
Tom (*looking at his watch; loudly whispering*) Twelve, eleven, ten ...

The others excitedly join in

Everyone Nine, eight, seven ...
Miracle (*suddenly standing*) Stop! Tricia needs to tell us something very important!

A pause. The children look questioningly at Miracle

Tricia You mustn't do this ... there's no terrorists. Miss Sheehan does support Arsenal. I don't know anyone from the head of British Intelligence ...
Anna Yeah, exactly. 'Cos Ben's the spy. Not you.

Pause

Ben Tricia's right. We're not spies. You can't live in the centre of the Earth, even with a suit of Starlite ...
Tricia The queen is probably not even a lizard ...

Pause

James It's a common problem. I've seen it many times in battle. They're cracking up under the pressure. Don't worry about it. Keep counting!
Everyone Five, four, three, two, one!

They burst in to the Crazy Frog Anthem

Miracle (*panicking*) My mum says that when you're feeling over-excited you should sit down and breathe calmly!
Matthew I thought you said you hate your mum.
Miracle I know ... and now I realize that I love her more than anything in the world.

Tricia grabs Sonny's arm as Sonny begins to sing

Tricia Sonny! You've got to stop them. You know I make stuff up all the time! Tell them! You're my best friend!
Sonny You're not my friend, Tricia. I'll never forgive you for telling Jenelle that I love her.

Everyone continues singing as Rab and James crawl to the front of the bus. They hide behind the driver each armed with a packed lunch box and a satsuma

As the children get towards the end of the third time through they begin to sing in loud, excited voices

Tricia
Ben } (*together*) MISS SHEEHAN!
Miracle
Anna Stop them!

The children tackle and tie up and gag Tricia, Ben and Miracle using ties, scarves and skipping ropes

Tricia and Ben catch eyes and stare at each other. Suddenly the other children charge towards the audience, shrieking. Sonny glances back at Tricia. He pauses for a moment, then continues running

They attack Miss Sheehan and the driver

James (*while attacking the driver*) Take that, you North Korean Funny Mentalist Jellyfish Lizard Nastie! Think you could fool us did you?

Suddenly it seems that the children are back on their imaginary rollercoaster, swerving and lurching. All face the audience, their faces full of fear and excitement

Rab Waaaaah!
Jenelle Woooooh!
James Wickeeeeed!
Anna Arrrghghhghghgh!

CURTAIN

FURNITURE AND PROPERTY LIST

On stage: Chairs to represent seats on the bus
Packed lunches, one containing satsumas (for **Miracle**)
Gameboy (for **Chrissy**)
Pencil (for **Ben**)
See-through sick bags

LIGHTING PLOT

Practical fittings required: nil
Simple lighting may be used at the director's discretion.

EFFECTS PLOT

Cue 1   **Anna** leaves   (Page 4)
               Electronic sound of a Gameboy

Cue 2   **Everyone**: "Shut up, Mr Bean!"   (Page 5)
               Sound of the coach revving up